Electricity

Graham Peacock

Thomson Learning • New York

Books in the series:

SOUND • LIGHT

HEAT • MATERIALS • WATER • ELECTRICITY

First published in the
United States in 1994 by
Thomson Learning
115 Fifth Avenue
New York, NY 10003

First published in 1993 by
Wayland (Publishers) Ltd.

Library of Congress Cataloging-in-Publication Data
Peacock, Graham.
  Electricity / Graham Peacock.
    p.   cm. – (Science activities)
  Includes bibliographical references and index.
  ISBN: 1-56847-078-9 : $14.95
  1. Electricity – Juvenile literature. 2 Electricity –
Experiments – Juvenile literature. [1. Electricity –
Experiments. 2. Experiments.] I. Title. II. Series.
QC527.2.P43   1993b
537'.078 – dc20   93-33258

J
537
PEA

Printed in Italy

Acknowledgments
The publishers would like to thank the following for allowing their
pictures to be used in this book: Chapel Studios *Cover* (*right*); Tony
Stone Images 5, 9; ZEFA 23, 29. All commissioned photographs are
from the Wayland Picture Library (Zul Mukhida). All artwork is by
Tony de Saulles.

Contents

Words that appear in **bold** are explained in the glossary
on page 30.

Light a bulb

How often do you use electricity? You probably watch television, go to the movies, and play video games. All of these use electricity.

An electric current is a flow of tiny particles called electrons. In most solids, the electrons flow quite slowly, but the electrical energy carried by the electrons travels at the speed of light. Electrical energy can come from a huge generator in a power plant or from a small battery. Electricity is very dangerous, so NEVER play with electrical outlets or plugs.

How do light bulbs work?

You will need:
- ♦ **a bulb (2.5 v)**
- ♦ **a battery or cell (1.5 v)**
- ♦ **aluminum foil**

Can you light the **bulb** by using a piece of aluminum foil and a **battery**?

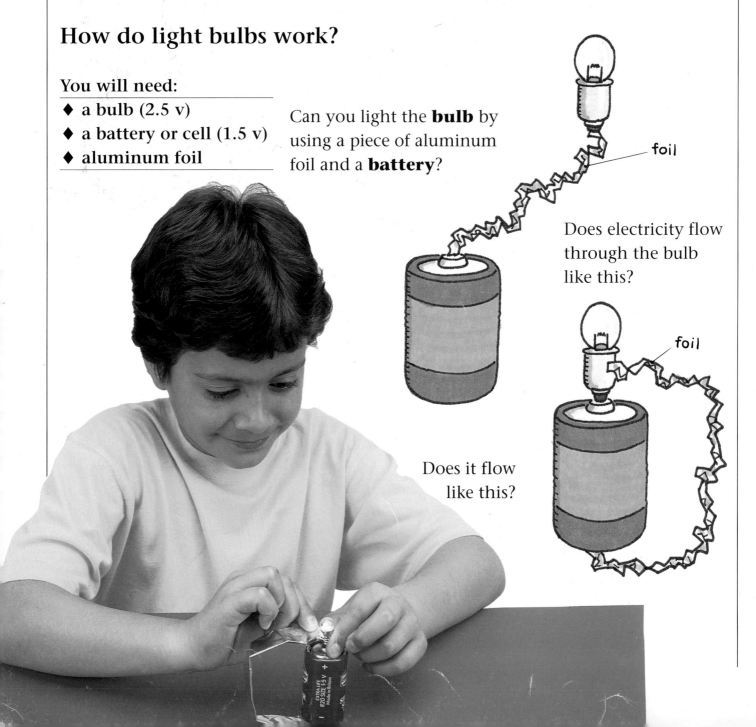

foil

Does electricity flow through the bulb like this?

foil

Does it flow like this?

How are light bulbs made?

Light bulbs come in many shapes and sizes. All bulbs made with a filament work in the same way.

Light bulb filaments are made from very fine tungsten wire. This glows white hot when electricity passes through it. ▶

Hot stuff

Tungsten wire in a light bulb glows at 4,500°F. Most other metals would melt at that temperature.

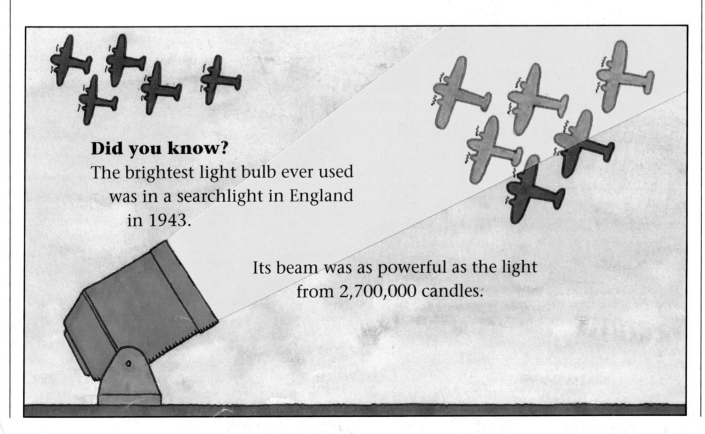

Did you know?

The brightest light bulb ever used was in a searchlight in England in 1943.

Its beam was as powerful as the light from 2,700,000 candles.

Handy sockets and switches

You will need:

- ◆ 2 wires (with alligator clips)
- ◆ a bulb (2.5 v) and socket
- ◆ a battery (1.5 v) and holder

1 Screw the bulb into the socket.

2 Put the battery in its holder.

3 Connect the wires like this:

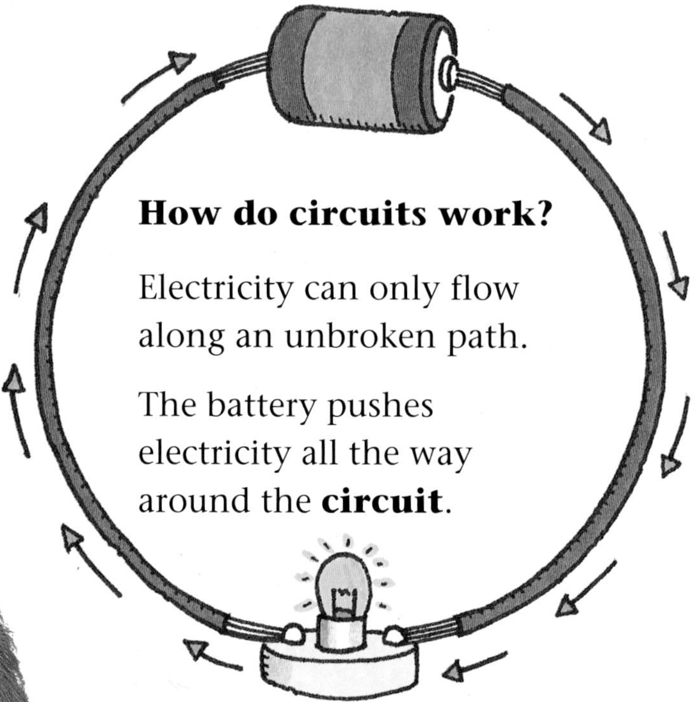

How do circuits work?

Electricity can only flow along an unbroken path.

The battery pushes electricity all the way around the **circuit**.

Voltage

The **voltage** written on a battery tells you how hard the battery will push electricity around a circuit. If you double the number of batteries in a simple circuit, you double the voltage pushing the electricity around.

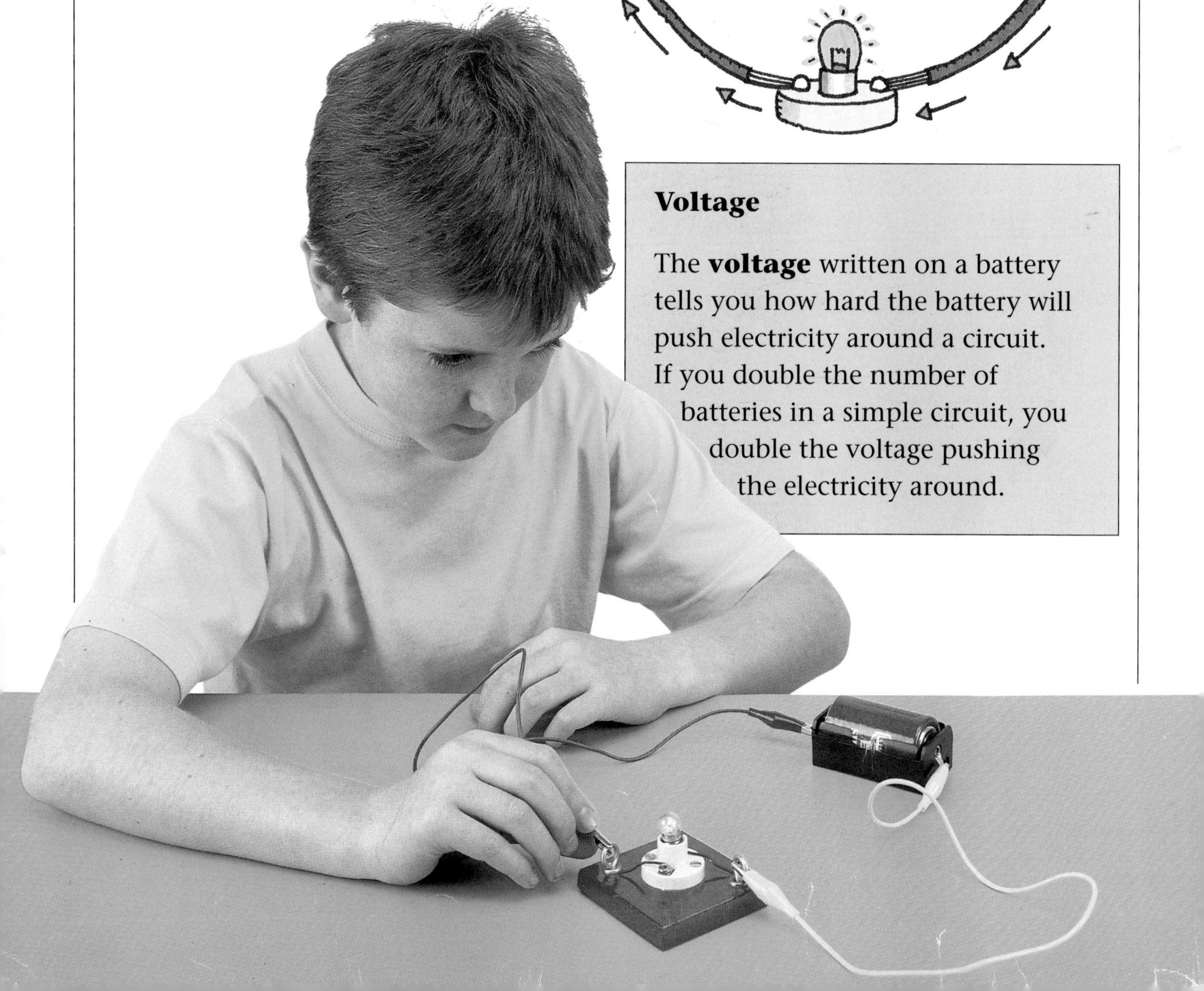

Turning off and on

You will need:

♦ simple circuit (opposite page)
♦ an extra wire with alligator clips
♦ tape ♦ foil ♦ thick cardboard

1 Add the extra wire to the circuit.

2 Make a **switch** by taping pieces of foil to the cardboard so that they overlap.

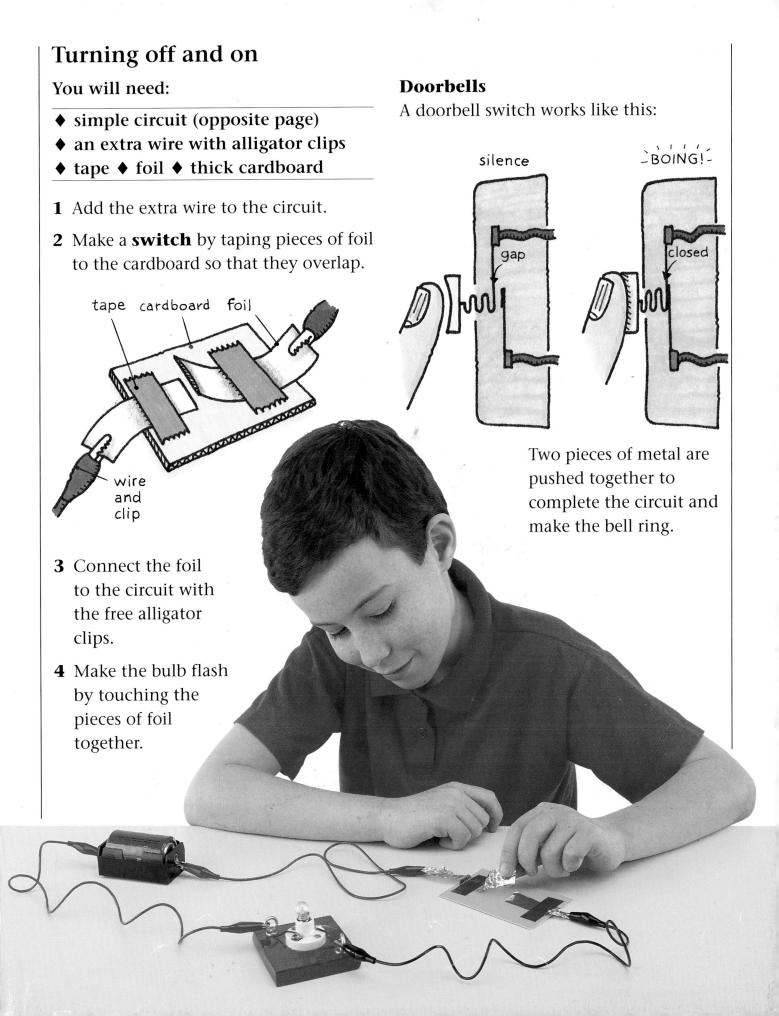

tape   cardboard   foil

wire and clip

3 Connect the foil to the circuit with the free alligator clips.

4 Make the bulb flash by touching the pieces of foil together.

Doorbells

A doorbell switch works like this:

silence   ⸱BOING!⸱

gap   closed

Two pieces of metal are pushed together to complete the circuit and make the bell ring.

Conductors and insulators

Which things let electricity pass through?

You will need:

- ◆ a battery (1.5 v) and holder
- ◆ a bulb (2.5 v) and socket ◆ 3 wires
- ◆ objects made from different
  materials

1 Make a circuit like the one below.

2 Test each object to see which
  materials let electricity flow through
  them.

Those which let electricity flow
through are called **conductors**.

Those which do not let electricity
through are called **insulators**.

All metals conduct
electricity. If they do
not, look to see if they
are coated in paint or
varnish.

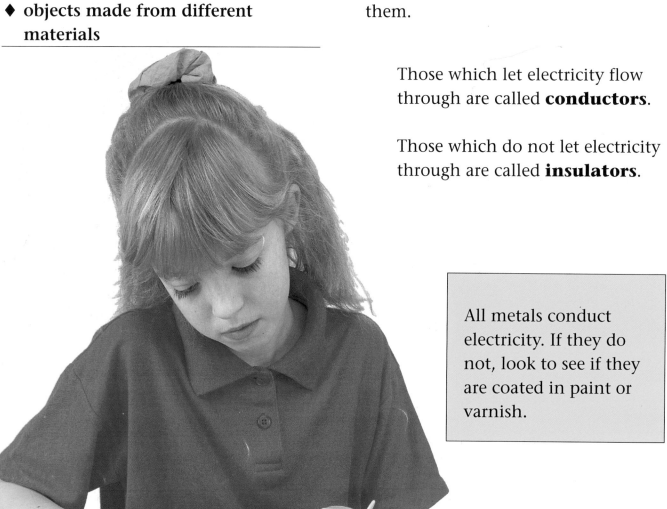

Using conductors and insulators

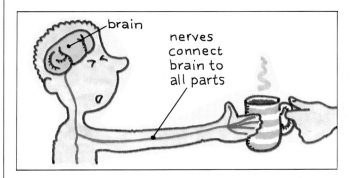

brain

nerves connect brain to all parts

Body electric

Your brain sends tiny amounts of electricity along your nerves to pass messages to parts of your body.

Did you know?

Gold is the best conductor of electricity. However, it is too heavy, weak, and expensive to be used for ordinary wires.

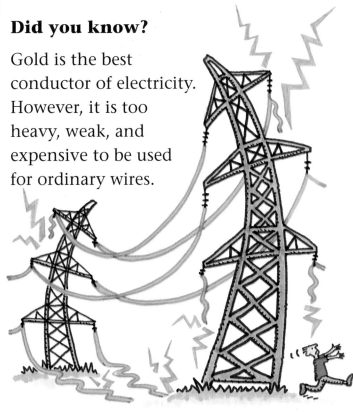

▲ *Pottery is a good insulator. It is used to prevent electricity from overhead wires from passing into the steel pylons that hold the wires. Aluminum conducts electricity well and is light and cheap. It is often used to make wires.*

The plastic case of the plug does not conduct electricity

It is very dangerous to touch the metal prongs when the plug is in the socket.

Plastic insulator covers the wire

Broken plastic can uncover the live metal wire.

Resistors

Cutting down electricity flow

You will need:

♦ a mechanical pencil lead ♦ a bulb (2.5 v) and socket ♦ 2 batteries (1.5 v) and holders   ♦ 4 wires

1 Make a circuit like the one below.

2 Clip the wires onto the pencil lead so electricity passes through it.

3 Move the clips closer to each other along the pencil. What happens to the brightness of the bulb?

Resistors

At room temperature even good conductors such as gold and copper resist some of the flow of electricity. Materials known as superconductors, however, have special properties that cause them not to resist electricity at all when they are held at very low temperatures (-235°F).

Will electricity flow through water?

You will need:

♦ a large container of very salty water ♦ aluminum foil ♦ 4 wires
♦ a bulb (2.5 v) and socket
♦ 2 batteries (1.5 v) and holders

1 Set up the circuit with the foil pieces as far apart as possible in the water, as shown.

2 Move the foil pieces closer together.

What happens to the brightness of the bulb?

Electric fish

The electric eel of South America gives out a powerful electric shock that travels through water to stun the eel's prey.

Wet hand danger

Although water does not conduct electricity by itself, many materials make good conductors of electricity when they are wet. Never touch anything electrical when your hands are wet – you could be electrocuted. Be especially careful in the bathroom.

11

More bulbs

What happens when you add bulbs to a circuit?

You will need:

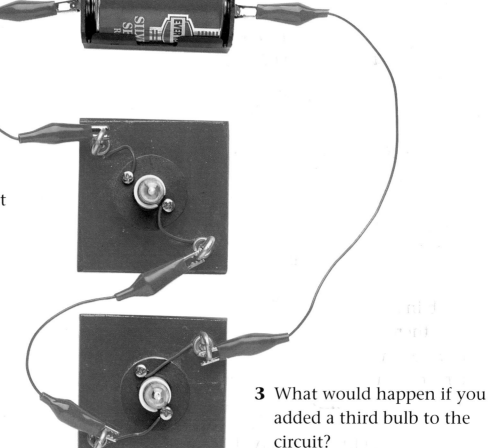

- ◆ 2 bulbs (2.5 v) and sockets
- ◆ a battery (1.5 v) and holder
- ◆ 3 wires

1 Make a simple circuit using only one bulb, as on page 6.

2 Connect the other bulb. What happens to the brightness of the bulbs? Do you know why this happens?

3 What would happen if you added a third bulb to the circuit?

Series

This kind of circuit is called a **series circuit.** In a series circuit the resistance from both bulbs cuts down the amount of electricity that can flow.

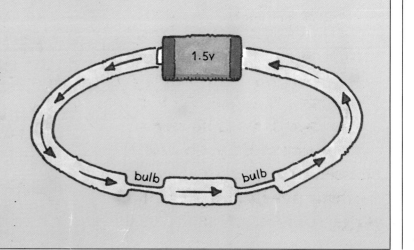

How can you keep the bulbs bright?

You will need:

♦ 2 bulbs (2.5 v) and sockets ♦ a battery (1.5 v) and holder ♦ 4 wires

1 Make a simple circuit (see page 6).

2 Add a second bulb to the circuit by joining it with wires to the first bulb as shown.

3 What do you notice about the brightness of the bulbs now?

How many bulbs can you add like this before they dim?

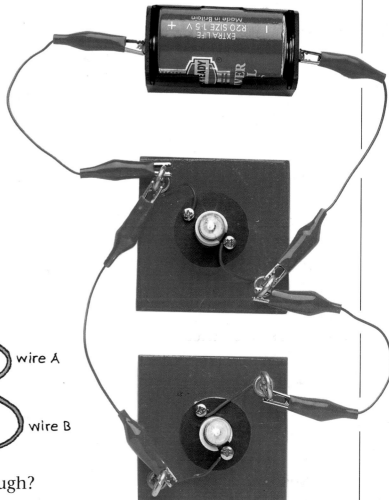

Short circuit

Electricity always flows along the easiest path. If there is no bulb in a circuit, there is no resistance to the electricity. This is called a **short circuit.**

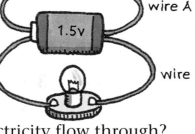

Which wire will the electricity flow through? The answer is on page 32.

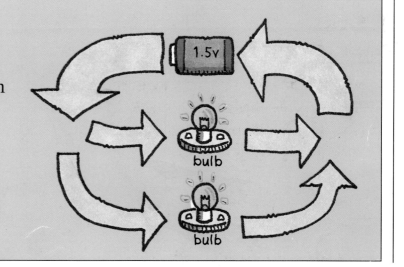

Parallel circuits

The bulbs on this page are arranged in **parallel circuits**. In these circuits the electricity can follow two paths. If the bulbs are the same voltage, there is the same resistance along both paths, so the bulbs are equally bright.

Electrical models

Can you make a model that uses electricity? Here are some ideas:

Robot

You will need:

- ♦ a cardboard box ♦ colored paper or paints ♦ strong tape ♦ glue
- ♦ scissors ♦ 2 batteries (1.5 v)
- ♦ 2 bulbs (2.5 v) in sockets ♦ 4 wires

1 Ask an adult to cut a window in the back of your box and two small holes in the front for eyes.

2 Decorate your box to make it look like a robot's head.

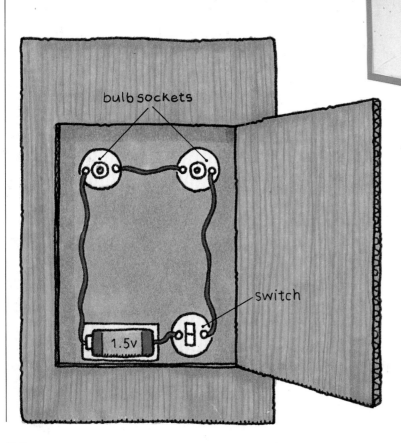

3 Tape the bulb sockets to the inside of the box so that the bulbs show through the eyeholes to the outside.

4 Wire the robot's eyes in series to the batteries. The eyes will light up. You could connect a switch (see page 7) to the circuit and make the eyes flash on and off.

Dollhouse

You will need:

♦ a cardboard box ♦ scraps of wallpaper and fabric ♦ 3 bulbs (2.5 v) and 2-inch sockets   ♦ 3 batteries (1.5 v) and holders ♦ scissors

Try to make one switch control all the lights.

Make a dimmer switch using a pencil lead as on page 10.

1 Decorate the inside of the box with wallpaper.

2 Turn the box on its side and put carpet or fabric on the "floor."

3 Ask an adult to make two small holes in the walls and one in the ceiling for lights. Push the bulbs through the holes.

4 Wire each bulb in a simple circuit with a battery. You could add a switch to each circuit to control the flow of electricity.

5 Furnish the house. You could use ready-made doll's furniture or make your own from cardboard boxes turned inside out and painted.

Traffic lights

Follow this diagram to make traffic lights:

Use colored cellophane to color the bulbs.

This is a parallel circuit.

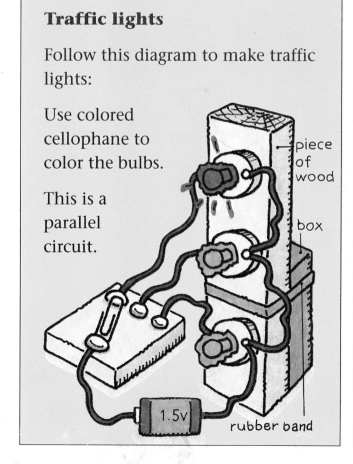

piece of wood

box

1.5v

rubber band

15

Electrical quiz board

Test your friends' general knowledge

You will need:

♦ a pen or pencil ♦ 8 pieces of cardboard ♦ 8 paper clips
♦ stiff cardboard ♦ 4 strips of foil
♦ tape ♦ a simple circuit

1 Write different questions on four pieces of cardboard. Then write the answers on the remaining pieces.

2 Use the paper clips to fasten the questions to the left edge of the stiff cardboard and the answers on the right, though not in a matching order.

3 On the back of the cardboard, connect each question to its correct answer with a strip of foil, trapping the foil under the paper clips.

4 Where two pieces of foil overlap one another, cover the lower strip with tape so that the foil strips do not touch.

5 Ask a friend one of the questions and touch one of the wires of the circuit to the paper clip holding the question card in place.

6 Get your friend to touch the other wire to the paper clip holding the answer card that he or she thinks is correct. If the guess is correct, the circuit will be completed and the bulb will light up.

How do Morse code signals work?

You will need:

- ♦ 2 long wires
- ♦ a short wire
- ♦ a foil switch
- ♦ a battery (1.5 v)
- ♦ a bulb (2.5 v) and socket

Connect the bulb, battery, and switch together in series. Use the switch to send messages to a friend in Morse code, making the bulb light up for long and short spaces of time.

Samuel Morse

Morse code was invented by Samuel Morse in 1838. He had already invented the telegraph in 1835. He wanted a code that could send messages along his telegraph.

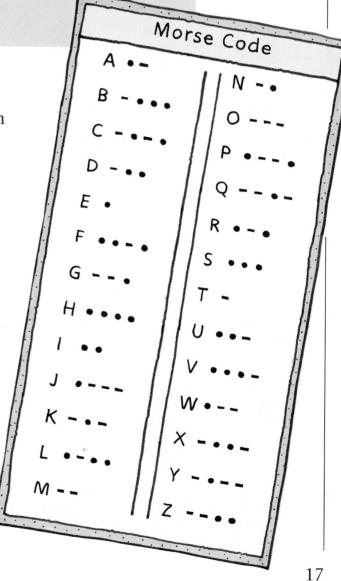

The first telegraph line was built in 1844 between Washington, DC and Baltimore, Maryland. Messages could now reach their destination almost immediately.

Morse Code

A ●—	N —●
B —●●●	O ———
C —●—●	P ●——●
D —●●	Q ——●—
E ●	R ●—●
F ●●—●	S ●●●
G ——●	T —
H ●●●●	U ●●—
I ●●	V ●●●—
J ●———	W ●——
K —●—	X —●●—
L ●—●●	Y —●——
M ——	Z ——●●

17

Burglar alarms

How do burglar alarms work?

You will need:

- ◆ stiff cardboard ◆ aluminum foil ◆ foam
- ◆ 3 wires ◆ a buzzer ◆ a battery (6 v)

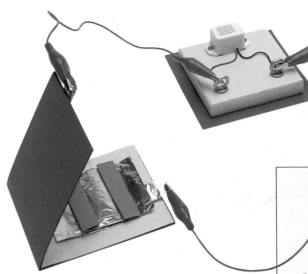

Buzzers

Most small buzzers only work when electricity flows through them in a certain direction. If you connect them in the other direction, they will not work. Most buzzers need at least a 3 v battery (or two 1.5 v batteries in a series) to work.

Pressure mat

Some burglar alarms use a pressure mat to trap burglars. The foam inside the mat holds the pieces of metal apart. When a burglar steps on to the mat, the foam is squashed, the metal pieces touch, and electricity flows through the metal contacts to sound the alarm.

Tilt switch

Some alarms use a tilt switch to connect the buzzer. Make your own tilt switch, using a ball of foil inside a cardboard tube. When the tube is tilted, the foil completes the circuit, causing the alarm to sound.

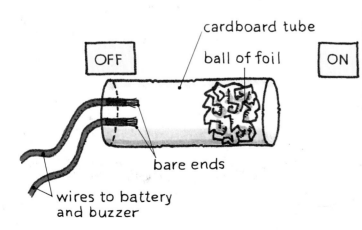

OFF · cardboard tube · ball of foil · ON · bare ends · wires to battery and buzzer

How do pairs of switches work?

You will need:

♦ 2 pieces of plywood or thick cardboard ♦ 2 paper clips ♦ 6 short strips of foil
♦ 6 drawing pins ♦ a bulb and socket ♦ a battery (1.5 v) and holder ♦ wires

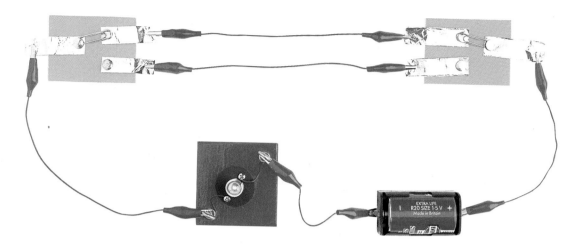

Make two switches and connect them in a stairway circuit, like the ones you can see above.

With a system like this, you can turn the bulb on at the bottom of the stairs, then off at the top.

Computer switches

Computers use groups of tiny switches to make **logic gates** in their circuits.

You can make two simple logic gates with pairs of simple switches.

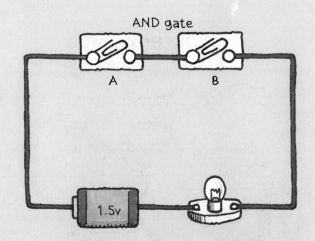

Both switch A <u>and</u> B have to be closed to make the bulb light.

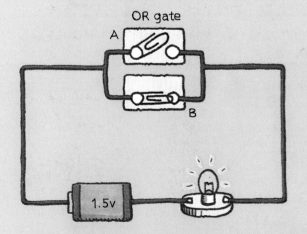

Either switch A <u>or</u> B will make the bulb light.

Light-Emitting Diodes (LEDs)

What are the red warning lights on televisions and VCRs?

You will need:

- ◆ 2 batteries (1.5 v) in holders
- ◆ a bulb (2.5 v) in a socket
- ◆ an LED ◆ wires

1 Bend the legs of the **LED**.

2 Connect the LED in series with the batteries.

3 Will the LED light up if you connect it in the other direction?

LEDs resist

LEDs need only a tiny amount of electricity to make them glow. An LED resists the flow of electricity.

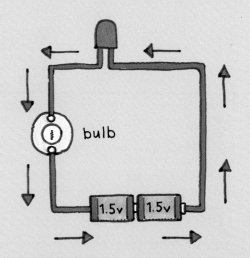

In the series circuit, the LED allows too little electricity to flow through the circuit for the bulb to light up.

4 Add the bulb in series to the circuit. Does the bulb or the LED light up?

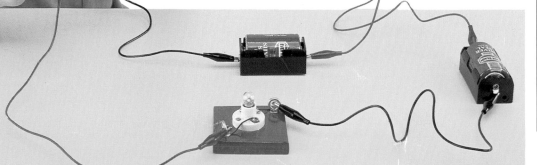

20

How do batteries work?

A dry cell battery consists of a zinc container, a chemical paste, and a carbon rod. A chemical reaction involving these three materials produces electricity. The battery stops working when all the materials dry up inside the battery.

In rechargeable batteries the chemical reaction can be reversed.

In this activity, the vinegar acts like the paste inside a battery. The metals and vinegar react together to produce electricity.

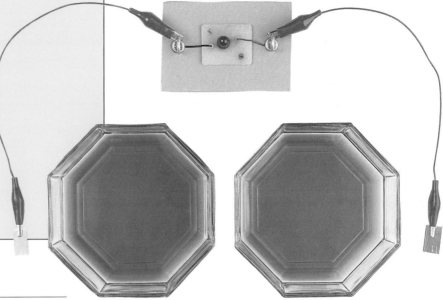

You will need:

♦ an LED ♦ 2 dishes ♦ vinegar
♦ 2 pieces of zinc (silver coins may work) ♦ 2 pieces of copper (pennies may work) ♦ wires

Set up the circuit with a piece of zinc and copper in each dish of vinegar.

If the LED does not glow, connect it to the wires in the other direction.

First batteries

In 1791, the Italian scientist Luigi Galvani noticed that a leg from a dead frog twitched when touched by metal instruments. Electricity was flowing between the metal and the fluids in the leg. The effect was seen by another scientist, Alessandro Volta, who went on to invent the first battery. He used stacks of zinc and copper disks, separated by fabric soaked in saltwater.

Lemons work as batteries just as well as vinegar.

Electricity makes a magnet

Warning! Disconnect the circuit when not in use. This is a short circuit and will drain the battery very quickly.

You will need:
- ◆ a small magnetic compass
- ◆ 2 batteries (1.5 v)
- ◆ wires (1 about 20 inches long)

1 Put the compass on a table. Keep it away from all iron or steel objects, including table legs!

2 Connect the batteries. Place the wire over the compass. What happens to the compass needle?

3 Disconnect the circuit.

Increase the effect

1 Put the compass in a small box.

2 Wrap the long piece of wire around the box several times.

3 Connect the wire to the battery and watch the compass needle now.

When electricity flows along a wire, it produces a **magnetic field** around the wire.

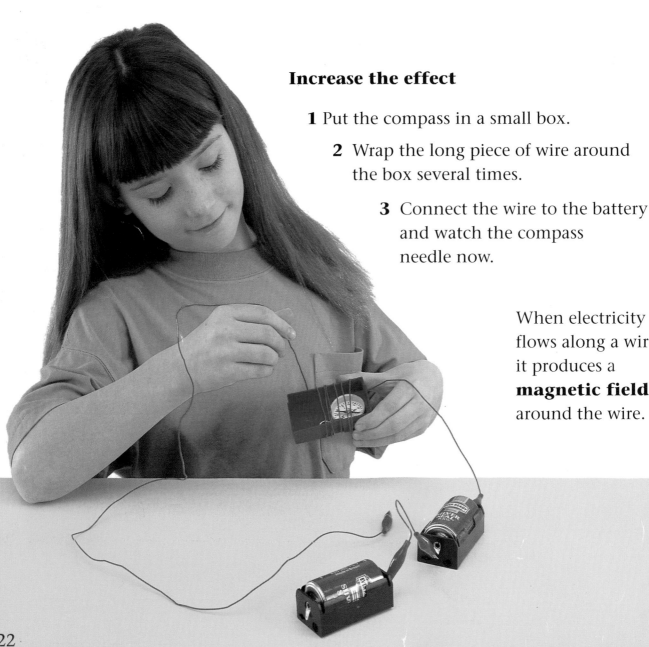

How do electromagnets work?

You will need:

◆ a large iron nail ◆ a long wire
◆ 2 short wires
◆ 2 batteries (1.5 v) in holders
◆ small paper clips or staples

1 Wrap the wire carefully around the large nail as many times as you can. Leave 8 inches of wire free at each end.

2 Connect the free ends to one of the batteries. How many paper clips can the nail **electromagnet** pick up?

Find out

1 Can you make an electromagnet by wrapping wire around a piece of wood?

2 Is the nail electromagnet stronger if more batteries are connected in series?

3 Does the number of times the wire is wound around the nail make any difference in the strength of the electromagnet?

number of winds round nail	number of clips picked up
5	2
10	4
15	6
20	8

Powerful electromagnetics are used to pick up iron and steel in scrap yards.

23

Electric motors

How do electric motors work?

You will need:

- ◆ a small electric motor
- ◆ a battery (1.5 v) and holder
- ◆ 4 wires

1 Connect the **electric motor** to the battery with the wires.

2 Reconnect the motor, swapping each wire to the other terminal. How does this affect the direction in which the motor spins?

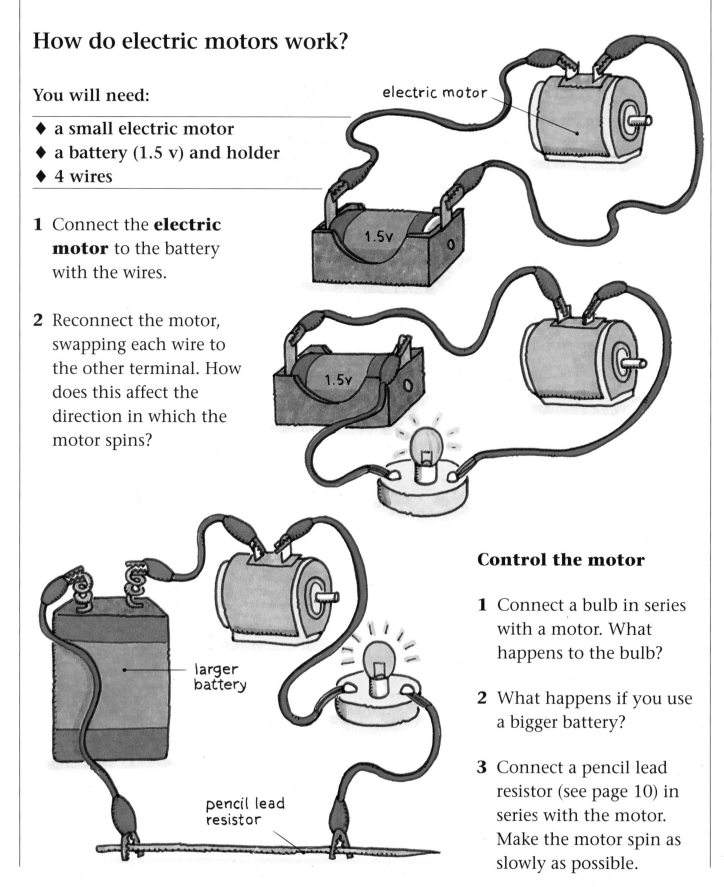

electric motor

1.5v

1.5v

larger battery

pencil lead resistor

Control the motor

1 Connect a bulb in series with a motor. What happens to the bulb?

2 What happens if you use a bigger battery?

3 Connect a pencil lead resistor (see page 10) in series with the motor. Make the motor spin as slowly as possible.

Make a motor

You will need:

- ♦ thin, flexible wire to make a coil
- ♦ 4 nails ♦ piece of wood ♦ 2 wires
- ♦ magnet ♦ battery ♦ wire strippers

1 Make a wire coil as shown below. Strip the plastic coating off the last inch of each end of the wire.

2 Push the nails into the board to make two supports, as shown.

3 Put the magnet between the supports.

4 Connect the nail supports to the battery.

5 Balance the wire coil on the supports over the magnet, so that the bare wire ends touch the nails. Give the coil a push to make it start spinning.

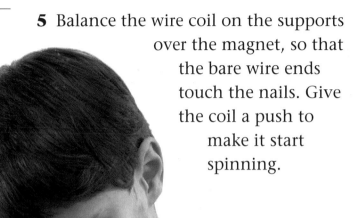

Repelling and attracting

The electricity flowing through the coil makes a magnetic field.

The wire is attracted to, then repelled by, the two poles (ends) of the magnet.

Static electricity

Picking up paper

You will need:

- ♦ a plastic comb
- ♦ small scraps of paper
- ♦ a dry, warm room

1 Rub the comb on your clothes or hair.

2 Can you make the comb pick up scraps of paper?

3 Find out which material is best to rub the comb on.

Jumping scraps

You will need:

- ♦ a cardboard box
- ♦ plastic wrap
- ♦ tiny pieces of paper

1 Put the paper scraps in the box.

2 Cover the box with plastic wrap.

3 Rub the plastic wrap with a dry cloth or your hand. What happens to the scraps of paper?

What is static electricity?

Static electricity is created when two things rub together. Although the electrons move from one object to the other, they remain within the objects, so are stationary, or static. The object keeps its electric charge until it is touched by a conductor, such as a piece of metal. It then loses its charge, usually causing a spark.

Static is a nuisance

Have you noticed a crackle when you take off wool clothes? This is static electricity that is made when your clothes rub together.

The plastic is negative because it has gained electrons

The fur is positive because electrons have been taken away

nylon carpet

If you scuff your feet on nylon carpet and then touch metal, you get a shock. This is caused by a release of the static electricity that has built up.

True or false?

1 Tungsten melts easily.
2 Electricity will only flow around an unbroken circuit.
3 If you double the number of batteries, you halve the voltage in a circuit.
4 Overhead cables are made from gold.
5 Your body uses tiny amounts of electricity to send messages to and from the brain.
6 Plastic is a good conductor of electricity.
7 In a series circuit the resistance of the bulbs adds together.
8 A short circuit is a piece of wire connected to a battery, with no bulb or any other resistance in it.
9 Samuel Morse invented the first battery.

Find the answers you are not sure of by looking through the book. All the answers are on page 32.

Charging balloons

Attracting charges

1 Blow up a balloon. Rub it on a piece of wool (or a wool sweater) to charge it with static electricity.

2 Hold the balloon against the wall in a warm, dry room.

3 Let go of the balloon. What happens?

Bend water

1 Rub a balloon on a piece of wool.

2 Hold the balloon near a slow stream of cold water from the faucet.

What happens to the water?

Balloon pick-up

1 Use your charged balloon to pick up scraps of crumbled Styrofoam, paper, sand, or dust.

2 Which pieces are most difficult to remove from the balloon?

Dusting

When you rub surfaces with a dust cloth, they become statically charged. This attracts dust. Many furniture polishes claim to reduce this static effect. Television screens get dusty because they have a static charge.

Repelling charges

You will need:

♦ 2 balloons ♦ a wooden stick ♦ cotton thread ♦ a dry room

1 Tie the thread to both balloons and hang them from a stick.

2 Rub both balloons in turn on the same piece of wool.

3 The static charge on both balloons is the same, so they push each other away.

Like charges repel.

What causes lightning?

Pieces of ice and hail rub together in a cloud, creating static electricity...

negative charge on bottom of cloud

Lightning jumps from the cloud to the highest object on the ground...

positive charge on steeple

A metal lightning rod takes the charge to the ground.

Did you know?

In Zimbabwe in December 1975, twenty-one people were killed by a single bolt of **lightning** as they sheltered in a hut.

Lightning flashes can be up to 20 miles long and heat the air around it to 54,000° F.

Glossary

Battery A container of several substances that produces an electric current by chemical changes.

Bulb A glass globe filled with a gas, such as nitrogen, and containing a wire filament. The gas keeps the filament from burning when it gets hot.

Cell A cell contains a carbon rod surrounded by ammonium chloride paste inside a zinc case. The metals and paste react together to produce a flow of electrons. Several cells together make a battery.

Circuit An unbroken path around which electricity can flow.

Conductors Substances such as metal that allow electrons to flow through them.

Electric motor A device that turns or moves when electricity flows through it.

Electromagnet A magnet made by passing electricity through a wire wrapped around an iron core. The magnetic effect of the electricity in the wire is increased by the iron.

Insulators Substances like plastic that do not allow electricity to flow through them.

LED (Light-Emitting Diode) An electrical object that gives off light when voltage is applied to it. LEDs are used on digital watches, VCRs, and other devices having electronic displays.

Lightning The spark that jumps from clouds to the ground when static electricity has given the clouds a much stronger charge than the ground.

Logic gates Combinations of switches that control the flow of electricity. Computers use huge numbers of tiny logic gates in their circuits to make electricity flow along different paths.

Magnetic field An area in which some materials are affected by magnetism.

Parallel circuit A circuit with two or more pathways for the electricity to flow through.

Resistor A material that allows electricity to flow, but with some difficulty. Carbon is a resistor. All materials except superconductors resist electricity to some extent.

Series circuit A circuit arranged so that electricity follows one pathway. The resistance of bulbs in a series circuit is added together.

Short circuit A circuit that has little resistance in it. One mile of copper wire without a bulb is a short circuit whereas four inches of wire that contains a bulb is not.

Switch Something that lets you break, then remake, a circuit.

Voltage A measure of the difference in charge between two parts of a circuit. The voltage between the positive and negative terminals of a cell is usually 1.5 volts.

Books to read

Asimov, Isaac. *How Did We Find Out About Electricity?* New York: Walker & Co., 1973.

Cash, Terry. *Electricity and Magnets.* Fun With Science. New York: Warwick Press, 1989.

Davies, Kay and Wendy Oldfield. *Electricity and Magnetism.* Starting Science. Austin: Raintree Steck-Vaughn, 1991.

Dunn, Andrew. *It's Electric.* How Things Work. New York: Thomson Learning, 1993.

Friedhoffer, Robert. *Magnetism and Electricity.* Scientific Magic. New York: Franklin Watts, 1992.

Parker, Steve. *Thomas Edison and Electricity.* New York: HarperCollins Children's Books, 1992.

Peacock, Graham. *Electricity.* Resources. New York: Thomson Learning, 1993.

Taylor, Barbara. *Electricity and Magnets.* Science Starters. New York: Franklin Watts, 1990.

Whyman, Kathryn. *Sparks to Power Stations: Projects with Electricity.* Hands On Science. New York: Gloucester Press, 1989.

Chapter Notes

Safety   The activities suggested in this book are tried, tested, and safe. Always remember: NEVER PLAY WITH HOUSEHOLD CURRENT. Do not use rechargeable batteries for these activities, since they may be short-circuited and get very hot.

Buying equipment   Although you can make bulb and battery holders from pieces of aluminum foil and cardboard, it is much better to buy equipment. You can get most equipment from small electrical dealers. If you cannot get holders for single (1.5 v) cells you may have to use a 6 v battery, but you will need matching 6 v bulbs. The best type of 6 v battery has spring terminals on top of the case.

Pages 4-5   It might be difficult to make this connection at first. The silver tip on the bottom of the bulb must touch the battery terminal and the foil must connect the screw part of the bulb to the bottom of the battery.

Pages 6-7   Always make sure your bulb and battery voltages are compatible. You are likely to break the bulb if the voltage of the battery is higher than that of the bulb.

Pages 8-9   All metals conduct electricity because they have many free electrons that carry the charge. In insulators the electrons are bound too tightly in place and cannot move.

Pages 10-11   The graphite pencil lead resists the flow of electricity, so the more graphite the electricity has to pass through, the dimmer the bulb becomes. Nearly all dimmer switches operate on this principle.

Electricity is able to flow through water because the electrical energy splits up the hydrogen and oxygen in the water. The particles of gas then have an electrical charge and flow to the terminal of the opposite charge.

Pages 12-13   The filament of the bulb resists the flow of electricity. When the bulbs are in series, electricity has to travel through twice as much filament, so it moves more slowly. This makes the bulbs dimmer. The position of a bulb in a circuit does not affect its brightness.

Pages 14-15   For the traffic lights, follow the path of the electricity with your finger, with the switch in different positions.

Pages 16-17   You can use wires instead of foil for the connections at the back of the board.

If you can arrange it, set up the Morse code equipment in two separate rooms.

Pages 18-19   Devise your own ways of triggering an electrical circuit. These can be in the form of simple drawings or in working apparatus.

Pages 20-21   LEDs are very cheap. All diodes allow electricity to flow in one direction only.

Page 22-23   The compass needle is deflected by the magnetic field created by the electricity in the wire.

Some electromagnets use bare wire coated in varnish, which acts as insulation.

Pages 24-25   Investigate an old toy motor. Inside you will see a rotor of thin varnished wire, surrounded by two curved magnets. One magnet face is a north pole and the other is a south pole. The magnets repel then attract the magnetized rotor, making it turn.

Pages 26-27   For these experiments, make sure all the materials are warm and dry. Mylar, used for covering books, produces a very strong static charge when it is peeled away from its backing material, and it attracts paper. Plastic wrap has the same effect.

Pages 28-29   Static charges repel each other when they are the same. They attract opposite charges. You may notice that sand particles are attracted to the charged balloon. When the two touch, they gain the same charge and so are immediately repelled, causing sand particles to jump back and forth between the table and the balloon.

Index

Answer to the question on page 13: electricity will flow through **wire A**, because it has the least resistance.

Answers to the questions on page 27: 1 false, 2 false, 3 false, 4 false, 5 true, 6 false, 7 true, 8 true, 9 false